Let Us Explore The Inevitable

Zorain Collier-Carter

authorHOUSE®

AuthorHouse™
1663 Liberty Drive
Bloomington, IN 47403
www.authorhouse.com
Phone: 833-262-8899

Published by AuthorHouse 07/23/2022

ISBN: 978-1-6655-6059-7 (sc)
ISBN: 978-1-6655-6058-0 (e)

Library of Congress Control Number: 2022909608

Print information available on the last page.

Scripture quotations are from the Holy Bible, King James Version (Authorized Version). First published in 1611. Quoted from the KJV Classic Reference Bible, Copyright © 1983 by The Zondervan Corporation.

CONTENTS

GIVE GOD THE GLORY
JESUS

SPECIAL THANKS TO

My Mother, who is totally responsible for my open and positive perspective on the subject of Death.

DEDICATIONS

- To my husband, Feltus Carter who has been my spiritual guide for the past 25 years.
- To my daughter, Julie Sanders, who I hope will greatly benefit from this writing. She has been so encouraging during the birth of this book.
- To my sister, Carol Motley, who has been my greatest and most helpful supporter all of my life.
- To my sister in Christ, Bernadine Gibson, who willfully converted this manuscript to digital.

ACKNOWLEDGEMENTS

Thank you to those who shared their experiences and thoughts after the loss of their loved one: Carol Motley, Zorain Holloway, Ashley Rhodes, Brenda Frank, and Derek Collier.

INTRODUCTION

One of the purposes of this book is to encourage the reader to explore death events in their lives to such an extent that they feel comfortable discussing it and the deceased person at any time. I want to inspire them to talk about the death of a loved one or close friend as easily as they speak of other difficult times in their lives.

Death is going to happen to all of us at some point during our lifetime, so let's talk about it. The time has arrived for us to bring the subject of death out in the open, and to form a more positive attitudes among our children early in life. Also we must address the fear, mystery, nervousness, and discomfort that so many people experience when faced with any death situation.

Birth is the beginning of life and death is the end of life on earth. Discussing death should and can be as easy as talking about any other challenging subject or event. This book can help you talk with adults and your children about death, dying, terminal illnesses and even suicide events.

This is not a manual on the care of a dying person nor is it a teaching vehicle on death and dying. It is meant to promote healthy conversation and experiences on the subject of death and to help those who are fearful or simply uncomfortable talking about the death experience in any manner, be more relaxed. It will detail the positives that death can bring as follows:

1) Death can end great suffering and despair
2) It can end severe pain and distress
3) Death can end misery beyond one's imagination
4) If an individual is a Christian, death can mean much more. It means to one day be with their Lord and Savior, Jesus Christ.

The more dialog on the subject, the more verse one becomes and that alone raises the comfort level. Therefore, it will automatically become a part of social conversation among many. For example, "Hey girl, what's new? Oh, I went to a funeral last week and it was most unusual. Really! First of all who died. One of my former co-workers, Ok, what was so different? It was a celebration of life not all of the sad stuff that usually occur at funeral.".

It is my prayer that after reading this book, people will take on a new comfort and a more positive perspective when dealing with the subject and the events of death because sooner or later it is going to confront each of us in one way or another.

"Let Us Explore The Inevitable," will also help the reader deal with the dying process and grief events. It can be helpful to families who may be caring for terminally ill relatives or close friends. Or find themselves in a situation that someone close has suddenly died, such as a suicide or an accident. Help for all of these circumstances are presented in this book.

CHAPTER 1

Starting at the Beginning

Mama, I am starting with you because you are where it all began. You set the stage for so much of my life. Although we had a stormy relationship, when I was a teenager, I thank God for the last 10 years of your life that we shared. We became church buddies and every Sunday was our time. It was breakfast before church or lunch after, it didn't matter. We were together sharing our lives and our God. Filling in so much of the many things I missed while growing up. As a child I wanted the two of us to attend church together. I would sit on the steps outside our apartment building and look across the street at all of the people going into that church and wish we were among them. It took years for this to happen and finally it did and I just thank God.

Scripture tells us that God (Isaiah 26:3) will give us the desires of our heart and He certainly did. I think we both recognized the situation for exactly what it was and we both appreciated it as such. There is a blessing in worshipping with your children. Mama, it has always been your fascination with death that opened the door to my involvement with the subject. I remember you taking my sister Carol, and me to view many deceased people when we were growing up. For you it seemed to be as natural as going to visit the living. You took us to a lot of funeral homes around the city, however, the one that stands out the most is the Metropolitan Funeral Home, located at 47th and South Park. The street is now named, Marking Luther King Drive. It was a very large place, and it had a lot of rooms. We would go to the desk as we entered and you would tell the receptionist the name of the deceased and they would give you directions. Once we viewed the body of the person we had come to see, you would peep out the door until the hall was clear, then you would take each of our hands and off we would go to view every deceased person in the place. I can recall how once we viewed five dead people without any interruption. My sister did not seem to be very interested, and sometimes you would leave her at home. I always wanted to go and found it to be fun.

The deceased people were always well dressed as if they were going to church. All the rooms had chairs in them for the people to sit around. I usually had a lot of questions and Mama you were so good about answering everything I asked and more. I learned a lot. Now I am grateful because it made death so easy for me to deal with. This has been a positive all of my life.

I remember when I started my first job in a hospital, as a nurse aide, I was so excited when I was assigned to take a deceased patient to the morgue and to assist with cleaning and preparing the body. A few years later while in nursing school and some of my classmates thought something was wrong with me because I was so happy when we students were scheduled to view an autopsy one particular day. I could not wait, while others were fearful, nervous, or busy trying to find a way to get out of the assignment.

At that time and for years later I could see that many of my hospital coworkers had trouble whenever a patient died. However, I was happy to do whatever was needed for the deceased patient. Whenever patients died in my unit or other units, I would volunteer to help prepare the body for the family to view, clean or take the body to the morgue. Whatever was needed!

I also enjoyed trying to comfort the family of the deceased. Mama, thank you for sharing with me a clear, comfortable and a positive lifetime perspective on the subject of death. And you spared me of not having the discomfort, nervousness, fears, or any other problems that so many people have when faced with death in any form.

Let's bring it to the table, the subject of death. Set your children's attitudes early in life about death. Instead of an attitude of fear and mystery, let it be an interesting part of life. Birth is the beginning and death is the end. Discussing death can and should be as easily as talking about any other subject. Make sure children know that it is the end of life on earth. Explain that when it happens to someone you know and care about, it will be extremely sad for a while, but life goes on!

Point out the positives: death can be the end to great suffering and, despair, the relief of great pain and distress beyond ones imagination. If one is a Christian, then death means that we will be with our Lord and Savior, Jesus Christ.

Once people start to have conversations about death, they will become comfortable with the subject and it may automatically be shared at additional social gatherings.

For example, "Hey girl, what's new? Oh, I went to a funeral last week and it was most unusual. Really! First of all, who died? It was one of my former co-workers. OK, how was it so different...etc.?"

This is not a manual on the care of a dying person nor is it a teach-all on death and dying. It is meant to promote healthy conversation and experiences on the subject of death. This book is to assist those who are fearful or simply uncomfortable talking about death or dealing with the subject. Hopefully, it will help families who care for relatives, friends who are terminally ill, or help people who are in a situation where someone close suddenly dies. Be better prepared and comfortable dealing with the activities such as the wake, funeral, repast, burial and talking about the death. The more dialog on the subject the greater the comfort level.

It is my prayer that after reading this book, people will take on a new comfort and positive perspective when faced with the subject and the events of death, because sooner or later it is going to face each of us in one way or another.

CHAPTER 2
Transition into Death

The dying process is as unique and different to each individual as is our fingerprints. Nothing is absolute. I think it is safe to say that we know as much about the end of life as we do about what it was like before we were born. I have watched many people die during my many years of nursing. I was always very concerned with my patient's state of mind. When their time of death was near, I took every word they uttered seriously.

If one is blessed to know their mortality, responses to death still remain as different as we are. However, there are certain generalize behaviors that have been noted in the research done on dying people. They may become isolated, refusing visitors, less interested in usual routines such as, watching TV, reading newspapers, being interested in current everts and hobbies. The dying person may begin to go down memory lane, looking over their life, relationships, successes, and failures, and many experience, "20-20 hindsight experiences." It is not surprising if some regrets are expressed or signs of depression may appear.

Accomplishments and other positives may be voiced as well. Excessive sleeping often occurs and usual activities come to a halt. Physically, there are often great decreases in appetite, which bring about a decrease in weight but the body takes care of itself. Although the person is not eating, no distress due to the lack of food is present and they are reasonably comfortable. Blood pressure decreases, pulse may increase or decrease or may become irregular. The body temperature may decrease and respiratory changes will occur. Close to the end, the dying person will talk less and less and will soon stop speaking altogether.

As the final day approaches, the person might undergo a sudden surge of energy and want to do a last-minute task of visiting with those they previously refused to see. This spark of energy is brief as the dying gets closer to death. Again, verbal communications cease, vital signs become irregular, Cheyne Stokes respirations, such as, very rapid breathing or very slow or even rattling may appear. As respiration stops completely, the heart stops beating, and the person has completed their dying process.

Why is it so important for family and caregivers to recognize the dying process? If family members or caregiver cannot cope with the process, they should seek assistance for the patient and find someone who can cope with the situation. Patients should be able to express their feelings and demonstrate their love without having to be concerned about others. Never attempt to force a dying patient to eat. It is not going to help if they don't want food and really don't need it. Don't try to make yourself feel better by getting them to eat food or drink beverages or water. They will not want or need food or drink, that time has passed. Those kinds of things are not needed now.

Many times family members are in denial about the fact their loved one is dying and is hesitant to accept it. Sometimes the hope for recovery is so strong they just do not realize that death is imminent.

CHAPTER 3
When Mom Dies

The death of one's mother is like that of no other. Your unconditional love has gone and cannot ever be replaced. The one tangible being who knew you best, had loved you most, and who loved you before you even knew life. She felt you in utero moving about, knew just what position to lay in to make you comfortable and which position to avoid so you would not be uncomfortable. You would respond by calming down. Mom attempted to eat all the appropriate foods so you would be healthy and strong and have an excellent birth weight.

She nurtured you through all the infant and toddler years, taught you many things as you grew each year. Mom talked with many people, did all the research, and learned everything she could about each stage of growth and development as you continue to grow. She was always mindful of all of your likes and dislikes as you continue to thrive throughout the years.

Mom gave you special attention, would actually study you to ascertain all of your likes, dislikes, desires and needs.

She remembered them and tried to fulfill them all of your life. She made herself the best source of reference for family and friends so you could always get whatever was needed for your birthday, Christmas, or any other special occasions.

When mom dies, we often feel as if much of ourselves has gone as well. And it's true because we never outgrow our need for her advice, her ideas, and personal thoughts on a great deal of what we do. Mom was the piece that held the family puzzle together. She talked to all of her children, her own siblings and other relatives in the family and helped to coordinate information and events. If you happened to be an only child, the bond can be even stronger and the loss may seem even greater. All of your life, it had been the two of you going places and doing many things together. She was your own private keeper and now she has gone. When mom dies, "It's a hard pill to swallow."

No one can comfort or nurture like mom. A mother's touch is always needed and wanted. Mom was your number one protector in so many ways before you were actually born. As great as the loss of mom was, and even though she will never return and can never be replaced, all is not lost. Hold onto the many cherished memories of mom, the traditions, and practices. She instilled her personality traits into the family. They came directly from her, both positive character traits and behaviors. Mom also instilled and nurtured you to develop into the good person you have become.

There is no quick recovery from the loss of mom. It is a slow and long ongoing process that can last over years. Most difficult to endure can be mom's birthday and Mother's Day. No matter how many years pass, strong remembrances may return and the desire to acknowledge or celebrate her.

Tears may come regardless of time passed. On the other hand, others may find it quite comforting to reflect on the experiences of mom's past shared birthdays. It may be even better and helpful to share old photos of previous events of mom with siblings and other family members.

I remember, for several years after the death of my mom, my sister and I would meet in one of the favorite eating spots of my mom. We would enjoy meeting on her birthday and sometimes would bring along some old photos to celebrate the occasion. A nice meal was shared but much more importantly, we were able to express feelings that helped (each of us) cope with our great loss. It was very therapeutic for bother of us.

However, while it is helpful to keep memories of mom alive and shared, it is also important to remember mom and events as they actually were. It is important to recall the good and the not so good. Don't focus on the negative, it is not helpful. But at the same time don't glorify mom. Don't make her into a martyr or saint. Keep it real! Let her remain as human as she was. Let the negatives go with her and continue to focus on the good memories, the fun events and all the joyful interactions. And over time, a lot of time, it won't hurt so badly.

After a while you will find that certain settings, especially holiday gatherings of family and friends, mom will often be a part of the conversation as if she was still around. **That is called keeping mom's memory alive**.

IT HURTS SO BAD

CHAPTER 4
It Hurts so Bad

The loss of a loved one or even a good friend is going to be hurtful so be patient with yourself. Allow yourself to experience the pain. Don't keep your feelings bottled up inside. Let others help you through this emotional maze. Seek out people in your circle who you know to be good listeners and then allow yourself to be expressive. These conversations can help you process and release feelings. Talk about love, loneliness, anger or even rage. Whatever is on your mind and hearts. You need to find a person you feel comfortable sharing those feelings.

Take a brief look at regrets or negative encounters you had with the deceased and you never got the chance to make things right. Forgive yourself and move on. Focus on love and positive memories of past encounters.

Throughout the entire grieving period, you must take care of yourself. Make sure you are eating healthy daily, even if your appetite has decreased. Maintain healthy exercise and sleep habits and attempt to keep your current activities as scheduled. During this time, the less changes in your life, the better.

Don't avoid talking about the deceased person. Find time to share with family and friends photos and memories of events they were involved in with the deceased. Utilize hobbies and other activities all of you enjoyed, such as going to the movies, out to dinner, musical events, etc. Stay busy with others as much as possible and don't spend excessive periods of time alone and in grief. Try to have fun, be cheerful in spite of your loss.

You cannot be up and down at the same time. You can't be happy and sad at the same time. So, look on the bright side during this dark time of grief. Remember to focus on all the joy this person brought into your life. The good times you enjoyed, the wonderful memories the two of you accumulated.

In order for one to be in a state of grief there has to have been good times shared to reflect upon. So, turn it all around and focus on the fun and happiness. Every time a sad or hurt feeling is experienced, and there will be many during this difficult time, again focus on all of the good and pleasant times. Surprisingly you will find that your grief period will be shortened in a very positive way. As my mother used to say, with such a bright affect, "You better wake up and smell the coffee while you can," (which means love, smile, forgive and be happy). People would say it made them feel better.

If you don't have enough family and friends that can help you through you grief, there is help available in most cities and towns. Support groups, grief therapy for very intense grief. Clergy and physician can also help.

Today, resources are so much easier to locate via the internet and social media. However, one must use caution when utilizing resources from social media and/or the internet.

CHAPTER 5
A Hard Pill to Swallow

When a loved one dies, no matter how prepared you think you are it will still be very difficult to digest.

When Elliot's sister, Sarah died early on Friday morning, he received a call from the hospital informing him of the change in her condition and his need to come immediately. He said, "Although we had been expecting this for quite some time, it was still a hard pill to swallow." His sister had made plans for her pending death. She made him the beneficiary of her assets because her adult children were unstable. The funeral arrangements, undertaker of choice and all of that was included in the pre-arrangements. But it did not make the situation any easier to bear.

The fact that the suffering was over really did not help. Sarah had been seriously ill for four years and her health was constantly going downhill. Thank God it's all over. All the pain is gone and I'm so happy about that but why do I feel so much pain in spite of feeling relieved?

Feel My Pain

Although I am praying daily for strength to get through the death of my loved one, I know God is keeping me and will comfort me. I know everything will be okay. However, I also realize my loved one will never surprisingly ring my doorbell again with one of her visits nor will she ever call me again. I can only look at the photographs I have because I will never see **her** again. It hurts so bad. I realize this emptiness will pass but for now I need to be surrounded by others who loved her as I did, those who miss her as I do now and those who can feel my pain.

After having experienced the death of my mother over thirty years ago, I know just how painful it can be and the many sequences of events that may be unexplainable. I recognize there are some things that will never go away. And I am aware that I will always continue to miss my mom. Only the degree of missing her will change and some remembrances that previously made me cry now, 30 years later, make me want to smile.

GRIEF

CHAPTER 6
Grief

In the early 1980's, I read a little book called, "Good Grief" by Granger E. Westberg. It identified ten stages of grief and explored ways to grieve well. I referred to this little book and shared it with many of my patients and most found it to be very helpful. Since that time, other authors have identified, "Five" stages of grief, and some have written about "3" stages of grief. However, experiences have taught me that the stages of grief have no set number or pattern carved in stone. Grief is very different for each individual. Being familiar with the various stages of grief can be very helpful to identify where one is in the grief process and how to work through it. A person must realize there is no specific order in which they must express grief.

Don't be alarmed if you think you have skipped a stage or you are in a state of grief longer than others were with the loss of their loved one. Remember grief is very individualized.

When grief occurs it affects every aspect of your life. It is a natural response to any major loss in one's life. *Matthew*

5:4, in the KJV Bible states: "Blessed are they that morn: for they shall be comforted." Grief will happen with the loss of anything tangible that is important to a person. Some grieve over the loss of a favorite celebrity, who they have never actually met. For example, movie stars, musicians, such as James Brown and Elvis Presley or public officials Harold Washington or Nelson Mandela.

Dealing with grief is difficult at best. It is part of life that everyone must encounter at one time or another. Grief may be caused by the loss of a great job, a house that was burned down to the ground containing all possessions or a car totaled while being unemployed and without auto insurance. All these are causes for grief. However, I think most will agree that there is no grief as profound to deal with as that associated with the death of a loved one. The grief process requires a lot of work. It presents itself in stages that are psychological, emotional, as well as physical.

It is healthy to grieve after a loss. The greater the loss, additional grieving can be expected and the longer the process may continue. Help keep the memory of a lost loved one alive by talking about them. The grieving person might find it difficult to stay focused or may have unfinished business with the deceased or maybe they have some regrets about their last encounter. Especially if the last encounter was negative. Allow the person to feel bad but don't let them dwell on it. Encourage the grieving **to** remember all of the positive interactions and let go of the negative. At this time it becomes very clear how short life is and there is no time for feeling cheated, robbed or being angry over past events. Grieving will not last forever. The person will soon be able to pull things and feelings into proper perspective.

The manner in which people deal with their grief depends on their religious faith. It can prove them either stronger and/or weaker individuals. Having seen many go through the loss of loved ones, I can confirm that the stronger their religious faith the better the outcome.

Take Care of Yourself during the Grief Process

During your period of grief it is vital that you take care of yourself mentally, emotionally and physically. The death a loved one is extremely stressful and many focus on dealing with the mental and emotional aspects of life but neglect to pay much attention to the physical. It is still just as important that the grieving person maintain a healthy diet and good sleeping habits. Address the changes in vital signs such as high blood pressure, rapid heartbeats, fatigue, dizziness, and changes in bladder or bowel habits which could be due to eating poorly. Also, loss of appetite may occur. All physical symptoms must be managed to maintain good physical health. Do not hesitate to get professional assistance for mental, emotional or physical problems that may occur.

While addressing all of this, it is equally important that you take care of your spiritual needs. No matter what your religious beliefs, you need to utilize them. Pray daily and often and utilize your spiritual leaders. This is the time to let God into your life as never before.

There is No Set Pattern or Rules or Format for Grief

Grief can be much stronger on the first anniversary of your loved one's death, on Mother's day or Father's day if it's the death of a parent. On your wedding anniversary if it is a spouse who has died or when the deceased one's birthday arrives.

One year ago, your loved one died. The time has passed so quickly, you can't believe it has been a year. But here are a few things that may make the passing easier.

1. Many people enjoy going to the cemetery to visit the grave site. You may want to invite a few special people to accompany you or make it a family affair. You may want to extent the event into a picnic or a lunch or dinner at the favorite restaurant where you and the deceased use to dine.
2. You might find it comforting to pull out the photo album and share with family and/or friends.
3. This may be the time to finish some incomplete scrap book or start a new one with old photos.
4. Make it a special day of reflection doing whatever was special to your loved one. The things the two of you shared. Remembering what was unique about the deceased.
5. Take a long trip down memory lane, just sit back, and enjoy it, either alone or share with someone else who also loved them.
6. Have three or more family or close friends gather and write out a list of a few things that the deceased

person meant to all of you. For example, always being helpful, providing support when needed, inspirational task, good company, etc. Allow each person five-ten minutes. Have each one shares their list. If the lists are long ask them to select two-three items from their list to share with the group and explain why these items were on the list. This exercise may be very helpful to everyone in the group. If done immediately after the death, it can be of great comfort to all involved. This exercise will possibly identify needs and bring family/friends closer together.

7. Never go there! Reframe from using statements such as "I wish I would have or I should have done this or that. It was meant to be. It was supposed to happen just the way it did." Try not to bring up the past. It is gone forever just as **your** loved one is gone forever. So, don't look back! Hindsight will always be 20:20 but cannot help or change anything. Leave it where it is, in the past!

Whatever event you select to do to commemorate this first anniversary after the death of a loved one, it will be extremely therapeutic if shared with others. If the deceased was a family member you may want to have a special party, lunch, or dinner just for the occasion and invite all of the significant people to share and heal. You are all survivors. An event such as this gathering will be very therapeutic for all involved.

No matter how much support of family and friends you may have around you even on a daily basis grief is a lonely, sad experience. You can have a "24-7" support system. Grief runs deep and is relentless. Therefore, it is important to take this fact into consideration when you encounter a person who is in **the state of** grieving. Be careful not to even so much as hint that they should just "Snap out of it" or expect them to end their sad state.

However, if the grieving person is a Christian, a comforter is available. In the book of Matthew 5: 1-4, Jesus assures us that "Blessed are the poor in spirit for theirs is the kingdom of heaven. Blessed are they that mourn, for they shall be comforted." So take refuge in Jesus, for He can greatly comfort us at this time as no other can.

Attached are a few Scriptures that will comfort and help us through periods of grief. There are many comforting Scriptures in the Bible and no comfort greater than prayer, reading and studying the "Word" at difficult times.

I assure you, "Jesus will fix it for you and everything will be alright. Being a good listener can be most valuable to a person grieving.

Scriptures to Comfort

- *Romans 6:23* - "For the wages of sin is death, but the gift of God is eternal life through Jesus Christ our Lord."
- *Romans 15:13* - "Now the God of hope fill you with all joy and peace in believing, that ye may abound in hope, through the power of the Holy Ghost."

Verses to Help through the
Death of a Loved One

- *Romans 6:4* - "Therefore, we are buried with Him by Baptism into death: that like as Christ was raised up from the dead by the glory of the Father, even so we also should walk in newness of life."

- *Isaiah 25:8* - "He will swallow up death in victory: and the Lord god will wipe away tears from all faces; and the rebuke of His people shall He take away from off all the earth: for the Lord has spoken it.

- *Isaiah 51: 1* - "therefore, the redeemed of the Lord shall return and come with singing unto Zion; and everlasting joy shall be upon their heads. They shall obtain gladness and joy; and sorrow and mourning shall flee away."

- *St. John 5: 28* - "Marvel not at this: for the hour is coming, in which all that are in the graves shall hear his voice. *29)* And shall come forth, they that have done well, unto the resurrection of life, and they that have done evil, unto the resurrection of damnation."

- *St. John 6:40* - "And this is the will of him that sent me, that everyone which seethed the Son, and believeth on him, may have everlasting life: and I will raise him up at the last day."

- *St. John 14: 1-4* - "Let not your heart be troubled: ye believe in God, believe also in me. *2)* In my Father's house are many mansions: If it were not so I would have told you. I go to prepare a place for you. *3)* And if I go to prepare a place for you, I will come again, and receive you unto myself: that where I am, there ye may be also. *4)* And whither I go ye know, and the way ye know."

- *Psalms 30:5* - "For his anger endures but a moment, in His favor is life: weeping may endure for a night, but joy cometh in the morning."
- *Ecclesiastes 3: 1-2* - "To everything there is a season, and a time to every purpose under the heavers: *2)* a time to be born and a time to die; a time to plant, and a time to pluck up that which is planted."
- *I Corinthians 15:26* - 'The last enemy that shall be destroyed is DEATH."
- *Revelation 21:4* - And God shall wipe away all tears from their eyes, and there shall be no more DEATH, neither sorrow, nor crying, neither shall there be any more pain: for the former things are passed away.

Grief and Grieving

- *Psalms 77.2* - In the day of my trouble I sought the Lord; my sore ran in the night, and ceased not: my soul refused to be comforted.
- *Ecclesiastes 3:3-4* - "A time to kill, and a time to heal, a time to break down and a time to build up, 4) A time to weep and a time to laugh; a time to mourn and a time to dance.
- *Romans 8:28* - "And we know that al things work together for good to them that love GOD, to them who are the called according to His purpose."

- *Joshua 1: 9* - "Have not I commended thee? Be strong and of good courage, be not afraid, neither be thou dismayed for the Lord thy God is with thee whithersoever thou goest."
- *Psalms 34:18* - "The Lords is nigh unto them that are of a broken heart; and saveth such as be of a contrite spirit."
- *Psalms 147: 3* - "He healeth the broken in heart, and bindeth up their wounds."

CHILDREN AND DEATH

CHAPTER 7
Children and Death

Let's not forget, we did not come here to stay! From the moment we are born our days are numbered. Illnesses, accidents, lifestyles and many other factors will shorten that unknown number but nothing can extend it beyond our designated time.

Let us begin teaching our children to have a different perspective about death. The first step is to share with them a clear understanding of the fact that, from the moment they are born, death is imminent. Death is on the way. The human body is declining in time and once it reaches its peak in adulthood, it starts to waste away physically.

If we are taught an improved perspective of death from childhood, we will be better able to deal with death and grief as adults.

Preparing Young Children for Death and Grief Experiences

Parents and caregivers of children need to first take care of themselves. And not only be in touch with their feeling on the subjects but understand the grief process. One of my favorite Radio Bible teachers, Dr. J. Vernon McGee, used to say, "Take the cookies off the top shelf and put them down low where the kiddies can reach them." That means make it simple so that even children can "get it!" This will really apply when dealing with the grief process.

Young children have many false ideas about death. Movies, television, and some video games complicate the subject even more. This is especially true when characters are killed and later turn up alive in a movie or game. This can be confusing for some young children. Parents and caregivers must make it clear to the child, no matter what their age, that death is the end of life as we know it. The deceased is gone forever and there is no coming back. The child will never see that person again. Death is irreversible.

Make it clear that death is inevitable. It happens to all living things including people. But with young children take it slow and use simple language.

I have learned from my own personal experience, like most things with children, if you start early in life the outcome will be easier for everyone involved and more positive. If parents or other caregivers will teach children at a young age about death, demonstrate a greater natural attitude toward the subject, and become comfortable about answering questions, their children's feelings will be more open and positive. There may be less discomfort whenever any death related event occurs. The more discussion the greater comfort! If parents are at ease with the subject of death perhaps the children soon will be also.

All parents and caregivers need to be prepared to deal with death on every level. One can seldom turn on the television without hearing of a shooting or a killing in our communities. Children are often involved. It is almost a daily occurrence in one place or another in our society. Everyone needs to be in touch with their view on death because it can hit home without a moment's notice. This will make them better equipped to help their own children, if there is a need.

There are additional factors that should be considered when assisting a child through the death and grief event. For example, the child's age and level of maturity, the relationship between the child and the deceased and the circumstances surrounding the death. There may be a number of environmental factors that need to be considered or addressed before the child is approached.

The child will need an empathetic, good listener who is also close to the deceased and that the child feels comfortable talking with. The person may or may not be a relative. A quiet non-judgmental listener who know not to add their own personal feelings with comments like: "yes, me too," or "that's right, I felt the same way," etc. Keep in mind the need to answer all the child's questions as much as possible.

Grieving is as individual as the rest of our behaviors so we need to let the children express their grief in healthy and safe ways. Allow them to have it their way.

Some Guidelines to Assist Children to Deal with Death and Grief

- All interactions with children about death and grief needs to be age appropriate and at the child's level of maturity. Explanations should be in simple language that the child can comprehend. This includes the funeral and viewing processes, memorials, repasses and any other services or events that may occur. Explain to the child what is expected and include terms such as, burial and cremation. Give clear and simple explanations as to what these events are.

- Be a good listener as you comfort them and keep in mind that all children will react in different ways to the death of a loved one. Some children may demonstrate no unusual changes in behavior. Other children may have many questions. Some may respond with big tears and long periods of crying or may be dramatic in other ways. Still others, especially younger children, may display some regress behavior such as bed wetting or may want to begin sleeping with parents again and express the fear of sleeping alone.

- A child, regardless of age, may need a lot of hugs and comforting. Console them as much as possible when they express or demonstrate the need.

- Encourage children to express themselves verbally. From time to time ask them what they are thinking and feeling. Ask them if they are having any dreams that are different from their usual dreams. Strongly promote expressions of feelings and try to pull out fears.

- Always speak to children in plain, simple language. For example: death is final, over for good, never to come back, gone forever and ever, never to be seen again, etc. Make it clear that death is permanent, that it is not a temporary status. Again, use simple terms and avoid statements like; "He/she has passed on," "we lost him/her," "crossed over." Don't use religious lingo, such as "he/she has gone home to be with the Lord," "gone to glory," "made their transition," "gone to heaven," etc. Be open and honest and don't hide anything. Listen carefully to any and all questions the child might voice. Answer as appropriately as you can because the questions may reveal to you more than meets the eye.

- Today's generation of children may encounter death in real life situations at a much younger age due to all of the gun violence in our society. So, while being supportive as possible never lie to them, no matter how "little and white" the lie may be. Utilize familiarity to make your point or share a story or answers questions.

- The death of a pet is an excellent time to introduce the subject of death and grief and help the child to deal with it. It would be a big mistake to quickly replace the pet with another and try to avoid the grief process and all the negatives that may accompany the sad event.

- It is not unusual for young children to think that they are in some way responsible for the death of a parent, sibling or even a close friend. Make it very clear that they are in no way responsible for the person's death. It is not necessary for you to always have all the answers. But always give reassurances.

- Help the child/children continue to build healthy coping skills and help them feel safe. Be watchful for mood and behavioral changes because they may still be experiencing grief.
- In small children, suddenly becoming fearful of being in the dark at night, baby talking, bed wetting and other regressive behaviors may occur.
- Comforting and reassurance must be ongoing, everyday situations.
- Try to keep the child's life as normal as possible.

Funerals and Other Services

In the event of the death of a family member or a close friend of the family, prepare the children to handle all that has occurred and the events that may follow. It will be necessary to talk to them in age-appropriate language about the funeral, repass, pre-pass, viewing, wake and any other activities.

After good simple explanations have been shared, whenever possible allow them to be involved in the preparation for the events, especially for the funeral.

Children may be able to assist with setting up for the repass or pre-pass, picking out photos for the funeral program, and any other small task. This will make them feel useful and relieve some of the sadness. Older children or teens may want to speak at the funeral services.

It is important to encourage the children to attend the funeral of parents or other close relatives and friends. They should never be forced to attend nor should they be restricted from attending any of the events.

It is vital that children be allowed to deal with grief and the death of parents, siblings, and anyone close, appropriately and immediately to avoid major problems later in life. Professional counseling is often needed and should be utilized if the need is indicated.

After the Services

After all of the preparations for the final going home celebrations are over, the viewing, funeral, repass and other services have ended, it's not over as yet for the family and certainly not over for the children. Visitors have gone and phone calls may have ceased. But the children still have a lot of needs. There may still be questions, quietness, loneliness, and maybe even still some confusion.

Maintaining on-going conversations, daily, weekly and even monthly are very helpful. You can encourage the child/children with supportive conversation. Demonstrate understanding as to how they **are** feeling. Don't try to hide your grief. Let them know that you are also hurting. Talk about the deceased person often and encourage the child to do the same. They may express more of their thoughts and feelings, which will give you a better idea as to where they are and how to help them.

Avoid surprises to the child/children, if death will cause changes in their lives. Discuss and explain any major changes that will occur because of the person's death. Assure them that they will continue to be cared for and loved.

It would be a big mistake to avoid talking about the deceased person. It can take many years for children to get over the death of a parent or other closed relatives. Some never really overcome. Help the child keep the memories of their loved one alive by sharing happy memories. Sharing days such as, Mother's day, father's day, birthday of the deceased, Christmas and other holidays and special days can make the pain even harder to endure. These days can renew the heart wrenching pain that seemed to have been getting better. So share only happy memories that can aide in the healing of the child at any time, but especially at more painful times.

As Time Moves

It is good to push children to honor their dead relative by living their lives just as their loved one would have wanted. Encourage them to enjoy life to the fullest. This is most appropriate for older children, especially teens but can be used for children of all ages as long as it is done with age-appropriate language and in a manner that also matches the child's level of maturity.

The death of a close loved one may bring on many emotions, such as feelings of abandonment, sadness, anger, guilt, helplessness, and others. Attempts at isolation may occur at any age. Some negative behaviors can be demonstrated by teens for example, alcohol or drug use and sexually acting out. These behaviors demonstrate actions of a teen attempting to find a new type of copying mechanism.

If the child's grieving interferes with any major aspect of their life such as, changes in appetite and sleep habits, decline in school activities or grades, or refusing to socialize with their usual friends are indications that professional assistance may be needed. It is very helpful if they can remain active with other children.

An Example of Why Children Need to be Educated about Death

Mom Help!

A nineteen-year-old college student called his mom while she was at work. He was seeking help for a difficult situation. Immediately upon answering the phone, she asked "what is the matter?" She could hear the stress in his voice. He stated, "I just got in contact with Jeffery." You remember him, she said, "of course." Well, I also learned that his mom died recently and I don't know what I'm going to say to him. Should I even mention it? His mom told him to offer his condolences, just be a good listener and let him lead the conversation.

It was a very difficult situation for both the young man and his mom because in our society so many people have not prepared their children to discuss death at any level. They often feel better to just "tip toe," around death events.

This teen has never had any closed connection with death or any serious conversations or teachings on the subject. Most teens and young adults are not sure how to deal with death when it suddenly arises.

This needs to change. We should begin early in our children's lives, teaching them and talking about death often at home. This will assure them more comfort when confronted with the subject.

Synopsis

Remember! As time passes children need continued support. This can be accomplished by using every opportunity to keep memories alive and sharing pleasant events and occasions that involved the deceased person. Helping them to recall the positives and fun times will aid in healing and getting them through the grieving process.

As soon as possible after death, take the time to explain death at the child's level of understanding. Make it clear that the deceased person is gone forever and is never coming back. Remind the child that the death of the person had nothing to do with them. It is important to explain that the deceased person had no decision in their death, and was not angry with the child or anyone else. And that no one can stop death. Explain to them, as much as you can foresee, what they can expect.

Whenever you see the child in deep thought or looking concerned, worried, or just lost, take the time to investigate. Talk to the child about what they are thinking or feeling at the moment. Stay close, be supportive. Let him/her know that all feelings are okay, normal and important and that the feelings may not go away for a while. See-saw the conversation! Listen to all sadness expressed but don't dwell on it. Change the conversation into something brighter and direct it into a fun activity such as, making a dessert or drawing a picture or whatever activity you know the child enjoys. Allow him/her plenty of time to go through the grieving process. It may be lengthy. Continue to focus on the fun and happy times shared with the deceased loved one. Help to keep the memories lovely and pleasant.

Another activity can be to create a list of all the things the deceased (grandma or dad or whoever) taught. Also a list of funny things the deceased person used to say or do. This can be a real fun activity. I did this with my children after the death of their dad. They were 14, 13 and 9. Their dad was a funny and fun orientated person who played with them all the time. So, the three of them really enjoyed this activity. Another was to draw a picture of the funniest things you and dad ever did. I provided first, second and third prizes for the winners. Every child won a prize. The first place winner got to select a prize first; second place winner chose the second place prize and the third place winner received what remained, so everyone got a prize.

Keep in mind, there are always trained professionals, such as, clergy, grief counselors, therapist, etc. They can assist with the grief process and maybe avoid some of the complications associated with grief in children. Remember children may experience sleep deprivation, poor performance in school, isolation from their friends, changes in eating habits or just life in general. If you see the need, seek assistance and utilize it.

Parents need to be prepared whenever young children begin to ask the same questions over and over again. You thought you had explained everything very well and they seem to have understood. Now they are asking again when the deceased person will return. Be patient and comforting.

Explain in simple terms that children can understand for their age. Refrain from making statements such as, "you'll see grand pa in heaven later. Statements like this can be unclear for a young mind no matter the religion of the family. Also stay away from euphemisms like, "he is sleeping in his grave" or "rolling around in heaven, etc. It is always best to be concise with children. Call a spade, a spade!

Be watchful of the child's play activities because children often act out their feelings in their play activities. If you notice any behaviors at play that are difference, investigate genteelly and as always be comforting and sympathetic.

Children must be given honest accounts of everything, age appropriately, related to the death of their loved one. Clarifications of any misconceptions must be made and more than anything else good listening skills needs to be utilized.

When my husband died, I had worked for years as a visiting nurse. My co-workers often called me the "Death and Dying Nurse." Many of the patients I took care of were terminally ill. In our office, others did not want to deal with death. Death was not an unfamiliar subject in our house, mainly because of my line of work and due to my involvement with death from childhood as explained in the introduction of this book. My 14 years old son and nine-year-old daughter did as well as could be expected with the sudden death of their father. However, my 13-year-old daughter, who was very close to her dad, had a most difficult time dealing with his death. The fact that it was so unexpected had a profound effect on her. With all of my experiences with death, I still had to engage professional help for her. This was 42 years ago and I am not sure she has ever really or completely gotten over his death. There is considerably more help available now than there was in 1976 when these events occurred.

My ten-year-old daughter was more concerned that I might also die. She frequently asked me health related questions. If I complained of a headache, she found the need to investigate and inquire if I was going to go to the doctor or take medication for it. She discontinued wanting to go to her girlfriend's house to play because she did not want to leave me. The night my husband died, my children and I were on an overnight Girl Scout camping trip. He had worked on the day we left for our trip so they knew he was okay! It was not unusual for him to not be at home when we returned on Saturday evening. We all thought he was out playing cards with his buddies, which he often did on Saturday night. The children and I went to bed as soon as we arrived home. I just knew he would awaken me after the card game. Instead, I received a phone call at 2:00 a.m. from his best buddy telling me he had just died in the hospital. I did not wake the children but told them in the morning, when much to their surprise their father was not at home.

My 14-year-old son understood. He had many reasonable questions and was a big help with both of his younger sisters.

I expected a display of many emotions from him, such as: anger, guilt, separation from friends or family, isolation, lack of interest in previous activities but much to my surprise, none of these common reactions to death by teens occurred. I could see that he was trying hard to act as an adult for his sisters and for me. So, I treated him as an adult. However, at the same time I was constantly talking with him and treated him as I would a co-worker in training. I frequently encouraged him to express his feelings and made sure I had more than enough time whenever, he wanted to talk. He would ask, "Mom, you got a minute?" I knew it would be at least an hour but the time spent was always okay and good!

Other coping mechanisms for teens: journeying, music, group activities, engaging in their favorite hobbies, verbal expressions to good supportive listeners, scrap booking, drawing, viewing photos and recalling past events shared with the deceased person.

CHAPTER 8
Prepare for it

Why shouldn't you have it your way?" You prepare for every other aspect of your life, even simple and far less important things and events.

There are many people who never thought about preparing their own funeral and even less about what will happen to their own bodies. They think more about their possessions. People often verbalize leaving various items to "So and so when I am gone." Some do prepare a living will after much encouragement. Others do it after witnessing fights and disruptions that occurred in families of others who have died. However, there are a few people who decide to do it for themselves on their own and a small number even prepare for it early in life.(Preparing for death is happening) more and more, which is a good thing.

Hopefully, the next step will be for people to begin to talk about their preparations and encourage others to do the same. I look forward to the day people will be planning their final days as they currently plan weddings or for the birth of their children.

I can remember the days when I was a young energetic nurse, working for the Visiting Nurses Association of Chicago (VNA). The supervisor of our office was responsible for assigning all of the patients whose cases came into the office for care. In the early 1970's there were 15-20 nurses working in that office. Hospice organizations were not common as they are today. When people became ill throughout the city and needed homecare, were dying and needed or wanted to be at home, many doctors and most hospitals would refer them to the Visiting Nurses Association Offices. There were very few private home health agencies. VNA of Chicago was by far the oldest, largest and most sorts after home health care agency in the city. VNA was very special to me.

Initially, I enjoyed working with very ill patients that continued to die. After a while I began talking with some of my nurse co-workers only to learn that most of them were not receiving terminally ill patients. Only a few of us were being assigned them on our caseloads. I went to my supervisor to find out why I was getting so many of the patients who were dying. She informed me that I was receiving the terminally ill patients because I was the only nurse in the office who seemed to welcome them and never complained. I seemed to enjoy and do well with them. I was flattered. The supervisor determined this by reviewing the daily reports. It was routine that all the nurses give a brief report of all of their patients each day before we got off duty. She would give us feedback, instructions, and directions, help us problem solve when indicated and even make changes if needed. This format was very good because at all times the supervisor was aware of all the patients assigned to the office. We received any assistance we might need.

I soon began to receive a full case load of only terminally ill patients. My co-workers affectionally began to address me as, "the death and dying nurse." I was comfortable with it and was never offended. Whenever some of my co-workers were assigned a patient who was going to die soon, they would try to trade patients with me for one who was not as close to dying. It was always fine with me, unless the patient lived out of my traveling area. That was the only reason I would ever refuse a dying patient. I worked with many, enjoyed it and learned a lot. It is very rewarding to know that you made a difference when so few were comfortable in dealing with the end stage of life.

CHAPTER 9
Advance Directives

Advance directive may be defined differently from state to state and also depending on one's personal views. The American Cancer Society states, "The two most common types of advance directives are the Living Will and the durable Power of Attorney for health care."

There are many resources available to assist with, living wills; do not resuscitate orders, organ and tissue donations, and many end-of-life instructions.

It is really important for you and very helpful to family members to take the time to make some type of advance directives while you are still able to do so. This will ensure that your wishes are carried out should you come into a position that you are unable to communicate them.

Advance directives are legal documents that permit you the opportunity to spell out your decisions about end-of-life care ahead of time and "have it your way," These documents are to address family, friends and health care professionals and prevent any confusion in the future.

Before beginning to put in place your advance directives, research to ascertain exactly what is required by your state. Most states require the document to be witnessed and notarized.

Most often the witness cannot be a potential heir or spouse nor the doctors or other staff of the facility providing the patient's health care.

The American Cancer Society suggests that there are many things to consider when writing a living will:

- Do not resuscitate orders, which are instructions not to use CPR if breathing or heartbeat stops.
- The use of equipment such as kidney machines (dialysis) or breathing machines (ventilators), etc.
- Whether you would want fluid (usually by IV) or nutrition (the feeding into your stomach) if you cannot eat or drink.
- Whether you want food or fluid, even if you cannot make other decisions.
- If you want treatment for pain, nausea or other symptoms or not. This may be called "comfort measures" or "palliative care."
- Whether you want to donate your organs or other body tissue after death.
- It is important to know that the difference between choosing not to have aggressive medical treatment is not the same as refusing all medical care. You may still get antibiotics, nutrition, pain medication and other treatments. The goal of this treatment is comfort rather that cure. You need to make it clear

exactly what it is that you want and what you do not want.

- You can change your mind, take back or revoke a living will at any time.
- Research your state laws. There is no general agreement for recognizing living wills from other states. You also need to know how often you have to renew your living will.
- If you spend time in more than one state, you should make sure your living will meets the requirements of all the states you frequent.
- A living will is much more limited than a health care power of attorney. However both apply only when you are unable to speak for yourself. But the living will takes effect only if you are terminally ill or permanently unconscious.
- A medical or health care power-of-attorney are types of advance directive that names a person you want to make decisions for you when you are unable to make them for yourself.

Different states may have different titles. A few resources for Advance Directives: American Cancer Society:

- www.cancer.org
- www.mayoclinic.org.livingwill
- www.UofMhealth.org.health
- www.gortsearch.com.

CHAPTER 10
Funeral Services

There is usually a great deal to do when a loved one dies, but don't try to carry the load alone. You are already stressed enough about the death itself.

When taking care of the business at hand, first select the people who can assist and soon after begin to delegate tasks:

- Check to see if the deceased person is an organ donor. If indicated, check their driver's license.
- Arrange transportation for the body of the deceased from the place of death.
- A.S.A.P. begin to seek the appropriate people to arrange the funeral.
- Factors to consider if known, 1) what is already in place, 2) what the deceased wanted, 3) what the family wants, 4) what is affordable and realistic and 4) what the other significant people are willing to do.
- Choose funeral home and cemetery, if not already stipulated.

- Notify all appropriate contacts and financial resources.
- Do you decide if you want to have the body present, the casket opened or closed, flowers contributed, and will donations of money be accepted are some of the major decisions that must be determined?

There are many resources available on the internet. It is a good idea to gather knowledge, current information, and prices before you select any funeral home for assistance. It is wise to shop around to select the appropriate funeral home, unless the family is set on a specific one, just as you would when making any large purchase as a home or automobile.

Often people elect to have a memorial service instead of the traditional funeral. A memorial service is the same as a funeral without the body present. Many holds memorial services in their homes or other designated places. The memorial service will really cut the cost of final expenses and may still be very nice and as complete as a funeral service. A celebration of life service is currently becoming popular in lieu of a memorial service. This service is frequently done after the burial or cremation. Again, this can really reduce the costs of services because it could be held in various locations.

CHAPTER II
Suicide

September 9-15 is Suicide Prevention Awareness Recognition Week. September 10th is World Suicide Prevention Day.

The purpose of these annual recognitions is to raise awareness of the need for suicide prevention. There are many childhood traumas that arise from physical and emotional abuse, death of a parent, abandonment, mental illness and/or substance abuse in the household. Regardless of the cause, children are very likely to experience health problems and/or mental illness in adulthood.

There are crises centers around the country that can assist. After treatment, over 90% of children no longer experience anxiety, abnormal behavior or emotional problems.

Suicide prevention activities help people become additionally aware and this helps to decrease the risk of suicide behavior. Statistics reveal that nearly 40,000 people in the United States die from suicide each year or one person every 13 minutes. Suicides exceed the death rate of homicides and Aids combined. Each year more people die from suicide than from automobile accidents. Suicide thoughts are a significant concern. However, the most critical risk factor for suicide is prior suicide attempts and mood disorders, such as, depression, alcoholism, drug use and access to lethal weapons.

Web MD explains the connection between suicide and schizophrenia, suicide, and depression and much more.

Prevention efforts seek to:

- Reduce factors that increase the risk of suicide thoughts and behaviors
- Increase the factors that help to strengthen, support, and protect individuals from suicide

Warning Signs of Suicidal Behaviors:

- Talking about wanting to die or kill oneself
- Looking for ways to kill oneself
- Taking about feelings of hopelessness and having no reason to live
- Talk of being trapped and/or being in unbearable pain
- Speaking about bring a burden to others
- Sleeping to much or too little
- Increasing the use of alcohol or drugs
- Withdrawing from people or feeling isolated

Additional Resources:

- www.journeyonline. org
- www.samhsa.gov/suicide prevention
- National Suicide Prevention Lifeline - 1-800-273-8255 (talk)

CHAPTER 12

Enduring the Death of Our Loved One Who Has Gone On

Death can be so very difficult for us. Sometimes, however, it may also be helpful, if viewed from another perspective. The more familiar we were with the deceased, the greater assistants their death might be for us. Remembering how they lived, their perspective on things and how they reacted to various situations will help if we are receptive.

Recall their former actions and their reactions, then think, "How can these things help me." How would (mom, dad or whoever the loved one was), have wanted me to handle this situation. What would they have done? You will acquire help relief in many instances and turn your grief into something different.

Let's look at the following situation and observe how one family dealt with the loss of a loved one after seeing that the grief period seemed endless for so many of their family members. They took a traditional family event and turned things around.

At the time, I was living in New Orleans, my friends knew I usually came to Chicago in late April for my birthday. They set up the planning for the picnic this year. The previous year the picnic had been cancelled because their family member had died a few months prior to the scheduled picnic time. So this year, I was not just invited but was firmly encouraged to attend. However, a few relatives were still uncomfortable about having a family picnic when, "the life of the party has gone on." I was informed that two close relatives refused to attend because they could not see it being fun with the life of the party gone.

About an hour into the picnic, after the greetings and welcoming was over, two young adults took the children and teens on an adventure trip through the park. I soon learned why they insisted I attend the picnic. Two other professionals with experience in the field of mental health were present. One of them worked for years as a grief counselor. We professionals decided that the grief counselor should conduct all the activities that were to follow and we would support and adhere to his directions. All went very well. There were ninety minutes of conversation about the death and dying of the deceased relative who was so missed on this day. Feelings were expressed, fears and concerns were explored, and even some periods of laughter occurred. The two of us assisted as needed but the grief counselor gave excellent suggestions to everyone who demonstrated a need. He summed up and closed out the session ten minutes before the young people returned from their adventure trip.

Immediately after food was served and everyone began eating, laughing, talking, and socializing as if it were a regular picnic. So much had been accomplished and the previous cool breeze that was felt over the picnic site turned into a warm, pleasant calmness.

CHAPTER 13
Dealing with Sudden Death

It's really hard after the funeral as everyone else's life seems to return to normal. But we are still going through. We must realize that just because we continue to suffer does not mean the people around us are also hurting or that they even realize what we are going through. Remember their lives go on as before.

Sometimes you need solitude after the death of a loved one. Family members may want to be with you at all times and never leaving you alone. If that happens and you realize what they are doing versus what you need, you must find a way to speak out. Perhaps a walk by yourself may be just what you need, resting at home or a visit to your loved one's favorite place may be a good dose of medicine for you. It may really lift your spirits.

It is important to recognize and deal with negative feelings, as well as the positive ones. If you feel betrayed, abandoned, anger, guilt, overwhelmed by work or other responsibilities because of the death, you must get help. Or if possible deal with it. "This too will pass." It is important to know in what ways others have the ability help you.

It is significant for your mental health to reach out to others for help as you identify your various needs. Assistance from those outside of family members can often be even more rewarding.

Ways to get through sudden death:

- Invite friends, relatives, and others to help you to identify a need.
- Find activities yourself to prevent loneliness from slipping in.
- Become a praying person immediately. No one can comfort like God. Prayer is a great help.
- Don't discontinue your usual activities if anything be more involved.
- If you have a church home/family, this is a great time to utilize them.
- Accept assistance and invitations offered by relatives and friends.
- This may be a good time to begin projects, hobbies, or activities you may not have had time to engage in previously.
- Don't try to keep things inside your home just as it was when your loved one was with you.

I knew a lady who kept everything in her home as it was before her husband died, even closet filled with his clothing. She maintained their bedroom just as it was and even his dresser with all of his personal items in tack. Everything remained until her family members, wheeled her out to a nursing home ten years later. Family members said she spoke about him constantly as if he we still alive. She obviously never learned to "let go."

"Let Go and Let God." Whatever your religious beliefs are, this is the time, as the hymn reminds us, to "Hold to God's Unchanging Hand." Faith will be of great value to you and have the power to strengthen you.

Philippians 4:13 states "I can do all things through Christ who strengthens me." If utilized, many support groups are available and can be very helpful. Your ministers or priest can also be helpful. Churches and other organizations have grief counselors that also have the skills to be helpful. No matter how you choose to deal with the grief process, remain aware that it is fruitless to deal with regrets. Never dwell on what if or what could or should have been done. Grief has no place for regrets.

Remember to leave the past in the past where it belongs. Nothing in hindsight has the power to change so move forward and keep all the positives and good memories.

CHAPTER 14
Testimonials

Following are brief testimonials from several people who have volunteered to share their experiences of coping with the death of loved ones. Their accounts of pain and despair, anger, dismay, disbelief, all the changes that grief took them through are very moving.

I emphasized with these testimonies because of my experiences with the overwhelming impact that death and dying can have on our lives. Grief can seem insurmountable, a cross we are doomed to bear for the rest of our days. We have a hole in our hearts that can never be filled, a wound that will never heal. However, as time passes, we may also realize that the pain has subsided, and we have survived.

In times of relentless grief, the knowledge that "…This too shall pass away …" may be the only thing for certain we can count on.

Mama and Best Friend, Carol Motley

In early August 1986, my mother was rushed to the emergency room, diagnosed, and treated for a severe bladder infection and released. In early September, after several wrong guesses and many tests, she was finally diagnosed with lung cancer, stage four. I believe Mama suspected cancer long before August but kept that fear to herself. Fortunately, her ordeal was brief. October 9th was on a Thursday in 1986. During the wee small hours of that day, at approximately 2:45 a.m., Mama died. Thus, began my long downhill journey into despair.

From a perspective of 32 years, it's impossible to recall the total impact Mama's death had on me. Memories of that fatal morning and the following days fade in and out like a slide show. I recall meeting my sis, Zo and stepfather, Bill at the hospital where she was pronounced dead. We stood around her body. I just stared in disbelief. My sister advised me to touch her, I recoiled. She gently took my hand and placed it on Mama's chest. I said, "She's still warm." Zo nodded. I touched her face and began to cry. I've always been grateful to Zo for encouraging me to touch her.

Funeral preparations and notifications kept the awful truth at bay during daylight hours, but at night grief kicked in and sleep was nearly impossible. Even worse, was waking up with that brief surge of relief, it was all a nightmare, than almost immediately realizing that it was true, not a nightmare. Mama was definitely gone.

I managed to keep my composure through the seemingly endless days between her death and the burial; through the wake, the funeral, and repass. On the morning of the burial,

I completely broke down at the cemetery. During the entire ordeal I hadn't felt as overwhelmed by her death as I did on seeing that casket, for the last time, and realizing that Mama was gone forever.

My boss said, "… take all the time you need." But I thought that staying busy and distracted would ward off grief. It didn't. Sometimes I felt out of control. Often, tears were triggered by a song, a photo, anything associated with Mama. I recall seeing her everywhere-as a passenger in a passing auto, facing the driver; at a distance, walking swiftly, merging into a crowd. I could tell it was her by the hairstyle, the coat, the way she walked. I also saw her in my dreams. Ironically, whether dreaming or awake, I never saw her face.

As our family's favorite Reverend, Pastor Green used to say, "Time will fix everything, and time heals all wounds." Well, I'm not really sure. In my case, the uncontrollable tears stopped, as did the imaginary sightings and frequent vivid dreams. The utter despair and sense of loss became bearable with time.

Today, three decades late, I can still get choked up when recalling a certain memory and hearing one of her favorite songs. But more often, such memories wrap me in warmth and smiles. I'm also amazed sometimes when I think of how I quote my mother these days…" as Mama used to say; like Mama always said…" There are many more.

All I know for sure, about the death of a loved one is that we may never get over it, after the grief, there is survival.

Da da, Gone to Soon, Ashley Bennett Rhodes

Just like any other morning, the first thing I did was head to the bathroom. Afterwards I decided to go back to bed for a little longer after all it was Saturday. Before lying back down, I glanced at my phone and noticed I had several missed calls. This was odd because it was 6 a.m. in the morning. It was also odd that my sister's mom called and left a voicemail at that hour. Immediately I realized the common denominator of the missed calls was my dad. I called the next missed call on my log. My cousin Lawanda answered and I knew something was wrong. Her voice was sad and painful. She said, "Uncle Dwayne is dead."

I've never lost anyone closed to me. I'm well aware that everyone experiences death at some point, but losing one of my parents was not something I foresaw happening so soon. My first instinct was to call my mom. I had to let her know, I needed somebody to console me. My mind was racing, I had just seen him; how could he be dead?

The entire family gathered at my grandmother's house that day. I felt sad because I'd lost my dad, but I was also hurting for my family. I was hurting for my grandmother, who had just lost her child, my aunts and uncles, my siblings, and my cousins. That night, we drank, reminisced, laughed, and cried a lot. In such an unfortunate moment, I felt connected to my family in a way I'd never felt before. That connection gave me a small sense of hope that I could survive this.

The first night was the worst and I'll never forget it. My sister stayed overnight, which gave me comfort because I felt like I needed her. She, my now husband and myself gathered in my living room on the couch. My sister and I cried a lot that night. Every time I closed my eyes I could see my dad standing in my kitchen, living room, in my bathroom. Like I said, I had just seen him.

My dad was not exactly father of the year. He was absent a lot during my childhood and he missed a lot of prominent moments. At a point in my life I was upset with him for not being there but that never changed my love for him. Eventually, I got over his absence and wanted to take advantage of the presence. I wanted him to really know who he had taken part in creating.

Easter was approaching and my fiancé and I had just moved into a new apartment. I was having family over for the holiday and asked him if he could paint my apartment. He wanted to complete the painting in the daytime, so I gave him my key. He'd be done by the time I made it home, so I told him to keep the key and I'd get it later.

When I made it home, he was still there? I sat in the kitchen to talk to him while he finished painting. This was a rare opportunity and it felt really good. I ordered pizza and grabbed a case of beer-the beer was for him.

My now husband agree to drive my dad to Union Station, so he could get home. It was late so I climbed into the backseat to sleep. When we arrived at the train station, I got out of the car to give my dad a hug. We said I love you and that was the last time I saw him. If I would've known, I would have hug him longer, made him understand how much I really loved him, or just stood there to get a last glance of his face.

After he passed away, I found myself crying when I thought I had cried enough. I would think I saw him in public, especially at church. Sometimes it was really hard to believe he was gone, because my entire life I would go weeks without seeing him. My heart wanted it to be like one of those times.

After a lot of prayer, talking to family, friends and reflecting, I'm in a space where I've accepted his death. Don't get me wrong, I still cry when I think about all of the moments he's missing, but the pain is different. His passing has taught me a few things, but the main takeaway has been to experience life and create memories with my family and friends.

Me, Missing Mother, Brenda Frank

The grieving began immediately. I was not ready to let her go, even after a long illness. I knew that her time at home with us had come to an end. I know I was being very selfish, but she is my mother and I love her so much.

The pain of my lost was so deep and lasted so very long. I prayed and went to work and tried to stay busy.

When she went to be with the Lord, I was not there with her. I felt I should have been there. In the day I saw her plot, it was a pretty July day and a cool breeze just came around my sister and me, and it was like, Mother was pleased with me. My heart felt a joy I can't explain. It was like a peace came over me.

As time passed, the hurt was easing. But I was still missing her deeply.

She had been a part of my life for 64 years. Calling her every day when I was not going to see her. Her phone number is still in my phone. I have not been able to delete it even though it has been quite a while since she left us. Tears are on my face as I am writing this. I remember seeing a lady who looked so much like mother until it felt like a bolt of lightning hit me right in the core of my stomach. That experience stayed on my mind for a long time. I am still just missing my mother. I tried to remember all the funny things about her and the things that I loved most about her. I just take it, "one day at a time."

To be honest just knowing that I will see her again. I know this writing is not finished, but I don't think it ever can or will be.

My Dad, the Love of My Life, Z. L. Holloway

My earliest memories are all around my Dad, expressing his love for me in so many ways. I was so proud of him. To me he was so handsome, smart, and strong. He was everything good. I was so proud to be Daddy's little girl. My Dad took me and my brother to Ringing Brothers Circus every October when it came to town. He would discipline us with a good spanking, when we needed it, so we tried hard not to do anything we should not do. Dad gave us an allowance of $5 per week. He was very protective of me and he was my hero.

Two months before my 14th birthday, my Mom, little sister and I went on a week-end Girl Scout trip. When we got back home it was almost midnight Saturday. At 3'Oclock my Mom awaken the three of us and told us to come into the living room. When I got into the living room, the first thing I saw was my Grandfather sitting with a serious look on his face. I thought something had happen to his wife,

Helen. Mom said to my brother, sister, and me that my Dad was dead. My brother fell out crying immediately. I could not cry; I also didn't believe it. It did not seem real. I could not grasp the reality of it. I didn't know how I felt.

Days later, my mother took us to the funeral home. I saw my Dad lying there dead, his hair line was not right. I felt his hands, they felt stiff. His face felt cold. I could tell they had sewed his eye lids together and also his lips. I knew every inch of him. But overlooking all of that, it was my Dad. I decided to take the numb approach so I did not feel anything.

My Dad died on May 9. One month later, it was time for my graduation. I was so upset and hurt that my Dad was not there. The more the summer days came and went, the more I realized that my Dad would never be back.

That entire summer was so hurtful and sad for me. Every song and seemingly everything reminded me of him. Oh, how I could have confronted him. To tell him how much I loved him. How I thought he was the most admired human being. Taking nothing away from my Mother, but with him, I was so proud of how much he loved me and made it so evident to everyone. I was never sure why he chose me, but I was so glad about it. Now the rug of my life has been pulled right from under me. He was gone from me. I grieved over my Dad all of my life. I cannot understand why he had to be gone from me. I am over 55 years old now and it has hurt me more than anyone really knew or understood.

It will be my privilege to die one day. The first thing I am looking forward to after seeing God and Jesus is being re-united with my Dad. One thing I can say is my Dad loved me during those 13 years enough to last a lifetime and I will never every say good-bye to him. I know I will be with him again.

Let Me Tell You, Derek Collier

Let me tell you a little bit about a man named James Douglas Collier. He was my dad. He was a tall, handsome man with a quiet, yet strong presence. He was a very no-nonsense type of guy and he had a specialized attitude about discipline. He wanted things done a certain way. And he was tough. He was very serious about his kids' success. He wanted us to do really well in school, and he made no bones about it. Especially, when it came to me. He had a very specific way of looking at the world and wanted to make sure that I knew it. He had certain rules for us to follow and he wouldn't bend. Like I said, he was tough. There is a hard truth for me to admit, but I was afraid of my dad. I loved him very much, but I also feared him. When he died I was 14 years old and I remember feeling, for the briefest of moments, a sense of relief. Then, almost immediately, I was overcome with a profound feeling of guilt. Guilt and shame for allowing myself to feel such a way about my father's death.

When he wasn't being a disciplinarian, dad could be a whole lot of fun. He was funny, he had the best laugh, and he made the best pancakes ever. We would play and laugh and eat a lot. He never fussed at us about anything. He would advise us on things that were very important. He said that we could have very bright futures, but we'd have to work very hard in school, get good grades so that working in adult life wouldn't be so hard. I like to think he meant it. He talked a lot about right and wrong. He even told me that I, as the oldest, and the only brother, was responsible for always watching out for my sisters. "I'm holding you to that, Derek." he would say. Then, when he had finished advising and teaching, we'd all watch TV, laugh, and eat. We really looked forward to the weekends.

Dad was a good man. He could be very stern and strict. He had very powerful convictions and I think he tried to live by them. I realize that, now. I also realize that he wanted so much for us, and that had he lived, my life would have turned out so much different. Perhaps, the hard lessons I learned might not have had to be so painful.

James Douglas Collier has been gone for a very long time. He was taken from us much too soon. I think of him all the time. I have only one picture of him and when I look at it, I can hear his laugh. I remember the way he looked when he smiled. I realize that life without him has not been good. I wasn't ready to be without him. I miss him so much and I know that it will be so wonderful to see him again, one day.

While Dad's death hurt, it really frightened me as well. Before he died I had never assigned any true value to death. I did not grasp the enormity of it. Strange as it may seem, dying may not have really meant much to me. I was only fourteen years old and did not have any personal experience with death. I had heard of people like Robert F Kennedy, Dr. Martin Luther King Jr. dying, but they were not close to me. It made me realized that I was also going to die one day and that really scared me.

Dad's death made me look at the world and myself differently. I thought more about my health, safety, and even my relationships with other people. His death made me realize that there was much more to this life and to think about the fact that I will one day have to leave. I had failed to remember where God fit into all of this. Back then, I forgot to recognize that life is God's gift to us. However, now I am aware of that fact and I am grateful. I thank Mom and my sister Julie for helping me remember how important and valuable God really is and how he feels about our lives.

Now I know that without him, the importance of this life is questionable, I am in no hurry to die, but one thing I know for certain, is that I am not so afraid of dying anymore.

ROB'S STORY

CHAPTER 15
Rob's Story

Rob is a 48-year-old government worker. He is married with two children. His wife is a well-known physician. Friends and neighbors describe Rob and his wife as the ideal couple. They are both active in church and their children's school events. Some say they appear to "have it all."

One summer evening, Rob was driving home alone when his car went off a bridge. He was instantly killed. Rob was not a drinker—nor did he use any drugs. He was very familiar with the route and always a very careful driver. It was thought by some, that maybe Rob fell asleep but that would be odd for him. All accepted it as a tragic accident until his wife found a lengthy suicide letter three weeks after his death. The letter was carefully placed where it would not be found immediately. In great detail it explained when and how the accident would occur. The why of the suicide was not released to everyone? Actually, only selected family members and very close friends were made aware of the letter. Most never knew it was a suicide. Rob stated in his letter exactly who was to be told and only them. His wife followed his instructions completely. Rob's adult children were not even told.

Two angry family members expressed they thought he was at times depressed. The two were told if they saw signs of depression, something should have been said or done. They, in turn, insisted his wife should have seen the signs or symptoms. The two remarked she was too busy with her career and children to notice what Rob may have been going through. Those family members who knew about the letter adhered to Rob's wishes so the letter and its contents were never revealed, and never mentioned again.

It has been explained that men often go to great lengths to hide their depression and thoughts of suicide.

ELLEN'S STORY

ELLEN'S STORY

Ellen, a hard-working professional woman in her early to mid-forties has two young adult children and a teenage son, a recent graduate of high school, is enduring a lot of emotional changes. Her adult son has married and moved to another state. Her only daughter already lives out of state and her teenage son is about to leave home to attend college.

Ellen recently sold their home and move into a small two-bedroom apartment. She need two bedrooms in order to have space for her son when he returns home for spring break, holidays and for the summer.

She has been parenting most of her adult life and accustomed to living in a large house. Now Ellen must adjust to a small apartment, a small amount of grocery shopping, and no extra meals to prepare. She thinks she now understands the meaning of "empty nest syndrome." Ellen is in good health, attends church weekly, has a number of friends and is usually very active with family and others.

Ellen remembers speaking about being glad when all of her children were gone so she could have some "me time." She would travel and enjoy herself doing exactly what she wanted.

However, it has been observed by those close to her that when not working, Ellen spends most of her time at home alone. She usually declined, when invited out and does not entertain or invite close friends over anymore. One friend wanted to give her an apartment warming, another suggested having a party to celebrate her son's departure for college but she declined both. Ellen's aunt shared with a cousin how she appeared to be sad all the time and now that she has time for her hobbies, she does absolutely nothing. The cousin remembered making a surprise visit and found her alone and seemingly unhappy.

Ellen's cousin asked her about food, she remarked, "there is no one to cook for anymore and I don't need much food." She appeared to have lost weight. Her closest friends and some family members noticed definite changes in Ellen but did nothing but talk to each other. Later Ellen reported that a neighbor, with whom she had no contact any longer arrived at her apartment early one morning and said, "You know me pretty well and you know I'm a believer in, if you see something you need to say something." A big confrontation occurred. The neighbor explained and identified signs and symptoms of depression. The reason for the early morning visit was a mutual friend shared several things with the neighbor that made her believe Ellen might be suicidal. The neighbor explained they could not let another day go by without doing something to help Ellen.

That visit led to a professional intervention. Ellen said the professional quoted some unknown author: "If you wake up and smell the coffee, your day may look a little brighter and your load may feel a little bit lighter."

Ellen had to admit her neighbor understood exactly what was wrong and saved her life. Decades later, Ellen is still so grateful to the neighbor for having saved her life.

A LETTER IN RESPONSE, TO VIVIAN

(Vivian called Zorain Carter early one Saturday morning. She informed Zorain that she had just buried her mother a few days before and she really needed to talk.) "1995"

CHAPTER 16
A Letter in Response, to Vivian

Dear Vivian,

I don't really know you very well, only through my daughter. She has spoken of you highly and so often until I feel as if I really do know you well.

Regardless, I can honestly tell you, I am sincerely sorry for your great, great loss! I can relate to what you are going through. I too lost my mother. I sometimes get so sad and hurt as though it was just weeks ago, although it was nine years ago.

A mother is the one tangible person who loves you unconditionally.

No matter what you did, mother is always understanding and cares even when the two of you did not necessarily agree. She cares about your side of whatever the issue. She is always looking out for your best interest. She cares about your every whim! And now she is gone.

Vivian, let me give you a few suggestions that may help you in the near future. Gather any and all personal items your mother gave to you, over the years, especially cards, letters and photos. If you are blessed to have cassettes (or video) tapes with your mother on them, then you are really fortunate. Get a few of her favorite things and keep them for yourself, such as books, trinkets, sweaters or blouses, etc. These items will later come in handy as a source of comfort, a pleasant thought or memory. This will happen after the hard! hard! and lonely grief has settled. I know it does not seem as if the hard grief will ever pass. But, it will.

You will have good and bad days. Your mind will be off of your mother at intervals but her memory will never be far away.

Allow yourself to cry as often as needed. Do not hold back. Talk as much as possible with relatives, your friends and the friends of your mother. They also share your lost and are in a state of grief over her death.

Do not avoid talking about her with anyone and don't try to do busy things to keep you mind off of your mother or the fact that she is dead, gone, forever until you two meet again in Christ, if you believe.

Focus on all of the positive things you can remember about your mother. I am sure there are many. Thank God, frequently, for all the years you had your mother. Many people are not as fortunate.

Do not dwell on "what if, if only or I wish I had." You cannot change the past so leave the past issues in the past.

Mother's day will be especially hard for you for years to come. If possible, avoid looking at Mother's day cards and gifts in the stores and Malls. Next Mother's day is going to be particularly hard because it is your first without her.

I can share with you later about how difficult and how to deal with it.

Now you must get through Christmas and just make it from day to day. Try hard not to blame anyone for anything in reference to your mother.

It will not help her now, and it is a waste of your energy.

I will be praying for you. Our Lord Jesus Christ can truly bring you peace. Believe in Him and He will comfort you. If you feel talking will help, call me anytime. You may even call collect if you need to, seriously, I care!

Sincerely,

CHAPTER 17
Wrap up Tips

- When talking about death or dying such as with people who are terminally ill, we need to be careful to always "keep hope alive." No matter how grim the situation may seem there is always hope. And even though the person is ill, they are still alive.

- We never want a person with a diagnosis of any kind to feel rejection, defeated, alone in the world, hopelessness or that no one cares.

- Give the person sometime to deal with bad news, whether it is a serious diagnosis, death or whatever. They may hear you but not really receive bad news.

- Our personal perspective is so important when it comes to dealing with death and the subject of dying. If it is a touchy, fearful or a subject to be avoided we clearly cannot help others. If this is the case, we need to work on ourselves and acquire the change that can assist others.

- It is very important, from time to time, to think about and actually have some discussions regarding our own death.

- Attempt to elicit a dying person's perspectives, fears and concerns when approaching the subject of death.

- Empathy must always be demonstrated.

- It is very important to remember that during a time of illness, grief or dealing with someone who is dying, it is necessary to be considerate of the primary caregiver. Everyone needs a break at some point. A little time to come up for air; take the load off and just to live for themselves for a while. The best time to deal with family issues is before a person dies. Make it clear by settling property, money and personal belongings, care of young children and anything else that is of major concern. If at all possible, find out in advance the desires of the dying person. This is so important!

- Family members of the deceased should never let "guilt" enter into the "grief work." It is usually displaced and does no good. So, cut it off the moment it surfaces with any family member. "If I had only done this or that." Tell them to stop. This behavior serves no useful purpose. Redirect them to a healthier subject.

- Death is final for the deceased person. However, life goes on afterwards. Remember the process following the funeral or memorial service. The deceased is buried and put into the ground forever. This is the end of the person's physical being.

As soon as possible and in most cases, the family will put away, dispose of, clear out, divide up and get rid of all of the deceased's belongings. Too soon after the funeral the deceased is not even mentioned by friends and associates when encountering family members. In many cases people avoid mentioning the deceased because they don't want to stir up feelings, or hurt the family members or talk about death. This attitude needs to change in our society. Hopefully, it will begin now.

Printed in the United States
by Baker & Taylor Publisher Services